Anna Roberts

THE CHRISTMAS ROSE

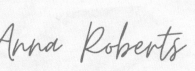
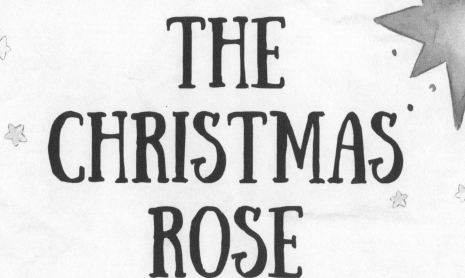

The Christmas Rose

The Christmas Rose (also known as the Snow Rose and the Winter Rose)(Latin name Helleborus niger) is a perennial herb that grows in cold, snowy mountains and high valleys across Europe. In the mid-winter season, the Christmas Rose blossoms when most other plants lie dormant and covered by snow. The pretty flowers are white and star-shaped and tipped with gentle pink.

Isaiah 9:6

"For to us a child is born, to us a son is given;
and the government shall be upon his shoulder,
and his name shall be called Wonderful
Counselor, Mighty God, Everlasting Father,
Prince of Peace."

On the first Christmas, God sent Mary her Son, and the baby Jesus was born in Bethlehem.

At the same time, Three Wise Men were travelling. These Wise Men studied the stars and knew a great deal about the stars.

They knew that at that time, all the world expected that Christ would come. And they had heard that when He was born, they would see a new star in the sky.

The Three Wise Men set
off at once to go and see
the newborn King.

It was a long way to go, and for many days they
rode across the sands on camels and travelled
on and on to where the star shone.

At last, they came to Bethlehem, and they went to the stable.

The Three Wise Men went in, and to their great joy, they saw the Baby Jesus and Mary, his mother, and Joseph.

The Wise Men were thrilled, fell to their knees and knelt in wonder and humility, and praised God.

On that cold winter night, while the Three Wise Men laid their rich offerings of gold, frankincense, and myrrh by the bed of the sleeping Baby Jesus, a young shepherdess named Madelon stood outside by the stable door quietly listening.

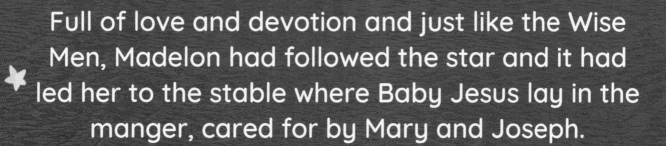

Full of love and devotion and just like the Wise Men, Madelon had followed the star and it had led her to the stable where Baby Jesus lay in the manger, cared for by Mary and Joseph.

And she, too, wanted to give the Baby Jesus a gift. But she had nothing to give because she was very poor.

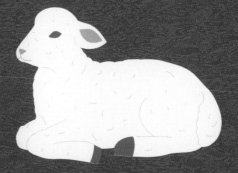

Realising she had nothing to offer, Madelon searched and searched the land to try and find one little flower that she could bring Him, but she couldn't find one single bloom or leaf because it had been a very cold winter.

Finding nothing on the snow-covered hillside, she became ashamed and began to cry in despair. As she cried, her tears fell from her face onto the snowy ground below.

As Madelon stood crying, an angel passing by saw her sadness.

The Angel came down towards her and, stooping, touched the ground and brushed away the snow at her feet. And there, on that spot, sprang up a bush of beautiful winter roses—waxen white with pink tipped petals.

The Angel told her, "No gold, frankincense, or myrrh, is as precious, or a more fitting a gift for the Christ Child than these pure Christmas Roses that are born from the pure tears of love, faith and devotion to our Lord."

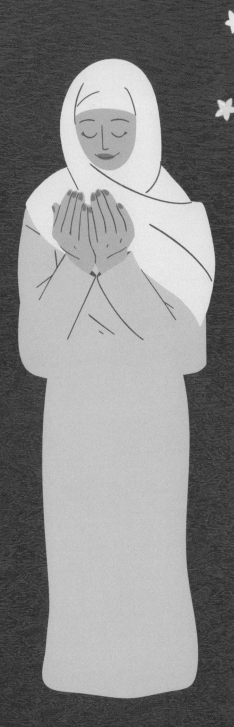

Madelon gathered the beautiful flowers and made her offering to the Holy Child, Baby Jesus, with great joy.

This is the legend of the Christmas Rose.

The End

Printed in Great Britain
by Amazon

14347676R00016